ODES OF US

EDITED BY

SHIRLEY JONES LUKE
EDDIE MAISONET

Published by Writers' Loft Press, Hudson, MA
The content of this anthology is the sole property of the individual copyright holders and may not be reproduced, distributed or transmitted in any form or by any means of electronic, mechanical, photocopying, recording, or otherwise, or stored in a database or retrieval system without written permission of the publisher.

Odes of Us

Shirley Jones Luke and Eddie Maisonet, Editors
Project Manager Kristen Wixted
Book Design Heather Kelly
Cover design Robert Thibault
First Edition
10 9 8 7 6 5 4 3 2 1
Copyright Writers' Loft Press, 2021
ISBN 978-0-9983172-5-0

For information about permission to reproduce sections from this book please write to: writersloftma@gmail.com
Visit our website for more information about The Writers' Loft:
www.TheWritersLoft.org

CONTENTS

1. Ode to Grace, Kindness, and Poets — 1
   Eddie Maisonet
2. An Ode to the Savoy — 4
   Shirley Jones Luke
3. Ode to the Harp — 6
   Shirley Jones Luke
4. Ode to Book Spines — 7
   Kaliisha Cole
5. Ode to Phillis Wheatley — 8
   Natalie Gonzalez
6. Ode to Cinnamon — 9
   Branden Ray Garcia
7. Kudos to My First Love — 11
   Alana Cooks-Beeks
8. Ode to Dad — 12
   Simone Jenkins
9. Ode to Jump Rope — 15
   Branden Ray Garcia
10. Ode to the Former Misfits — 17
    Aaliyah Beato-Hubbard
11. True African Beauty — 19
    Rebekah Davilmar
12. The Mirror — 23
    Ethan Mitchell
13. An Ode to my Errors — 25
    Emily Wu
14. Ode to Money — 26
    Rhoda Kaddu
15. Ode to Dreams — 27
    Ari Renzi-Surprenant
16. Ode to That Which Cannot Be Known — 28
    Sarah Saeed
17. Ode to Mofongo — 30
    Branden Ray Garcia
18. An Ode To Fighting — 34
    Adrianna Diaz
19. An Ode To Depression — 36
    Adrianna Diaz

20. Ode to Sappho: On Heaven 38
Natalie Gonzalez
21. Ode to Ebonics 40
Shirley Jones Luke
End Note 42

Other Writers' Loft Press Anthologies 45

ODES OF US

"POETRY IS NOT A LUXURY"
AUDRE LORDE, (1985)

∼

"For there are no new ideas. There are only new ways of making them felt, of examining what our ideas really mean (feel like) on Sunday morning at 7 AM, after brunch, during wild love, making war, giving birth; while we suffer the old longings, battle the old warnings and fears of being silent and impotent and alone, while tasting our new possibilities and strengths."

Ode to Grace, Kindness, and Poets

By Eddie Maisonet

Almost felt frivolous to center poetry
when there were grants, applications, cover letters, budgets to be written.
The voice called itself reasonable, but made no room for thriving only surviving.

The experience of being trusted with precious, vulnerable words-

   as a stranger,
   over email and Docs-

was something my spirit needed.
Cut through to the truth,
through the voice.

The narrative is harshly critical, unforgiving.
He understands the kind of year I had,
yet the voice makes no room for any kind of slack.
I work against him every day, to bring in
nurturing for the sake of nurturing.
To center joy.

These young poets remind me of my "why"
why I need to write
why I need to share
why I need to take in others' poetry
why I need poetry community

why gratitude is key to appreciate
poetry's transformation
of how being a person feels.

Poets, your work is beyond impressive
and you should be beyond proud of yourselves.
Some of you work, some of you live with illnesses,
some of you are preparing for college.
All of you have full, complex and dynamic lives.
Yet I had the pleasure of walking with you
as we shaped together something,
I hope,
you will be proud of—
a personal win for 2021.

It was brave to take on emotional work,
when you had every reason to slow down.
I celebrate your emotions.
I celebrate your journeys.
I celebrate your growth.
I celebrate your ability to feel difficult emotions.
I celebrate your moments of joy.
I celebrate your kindness.

Grace and forgiveness are hard to find.
Yet every single frantic email,
you offered grace and understanding.
"Life" kept happening for me
and you were kind, always.
Your poems danced alive like fire, spat truths,
gifted laughs, released tears.
What a glorious purpose to be a part of.

Kristen, Shirley, Writers Loft Press,
I will cherish your kindness and your warmth.

I look forward to holding the book we helped create.
Thank you for this opportunity to
grow as an editor
and luxuriate in being a poet
when I desperately needed it.

To say I am grateful to you is just the beginning
of how I feel.
Please, just keep writing, even if just for you.
I am thrilled for all you have yet to say.

∼

An Ode to the Savoy

By Shirley Jones Luke

No club like the Savoy

putting Harlem in a trance

Hope you can get in

swing, daddy, swing

move your body and dance.

Lenox Avenue was the place to view

fine men in rare form

women holding their heads high

ready to shake a thigh

it's all anyone wanted to do.

Do you hear the melodies?

sweet voices, putting everyone at ease

the stage is set, horns are blowing

I'd come to this place even in

the snow

I'm where I belong

a club like no other

trying to groove

and get to know each other's

moves & dance all night long

Savoy, you were a joy,

my heart longs for your rooms

music flowing, such eclectic tunes

rhythm makes me swoon,

when day breaks

it over too soon.

Ode to the Harp

By Shirley Jones Luke

A woman speaks,

her mouth an "O",

a woman

speaks her lips shape

the sound, her fingers strum

creates vibrations.

A harp can heal,

represents the gentleness of a woman.

A harp can hurt,

sharp strings, taunt from focus.

A harp creates a purposeful sound

as it sits on her lap,

her embrace cradles the instrument

and hopes a breeze

engulfs its strings,

a melody is born

that begins a symphony

Ode to Book Spines

By Kaliisha Cole

    Dazzling typographies splayed against various colors
    Different amongst others
    The fortitude of my shelves
    A collection of backbones

    Pushed together, a work of art
    Without a brush or pallet
    Divided into sections
    Various selections

    Worlds waiting to be explored
    A striking title to draw me in
    Flirting with me from across the room
    Waiting for the day that I choose you

    Marvelous spines that are more beautiful than jewels
    I'll admire you all from the place I sit
    Together, you are a puzzle
    And each of you have a spot to fit.

Ode to Phillis Wheatley

By Natalie Gonzalez

On Being Brought from Africa to America
By Phillis Wheatley

'Twas mercy brought me from my *Pagan* land,
Taught my benighted soul to understand
That there's a God, that there's a *Saviour* too:
Once I redemption neither sought nor knew.
Some view our sable race with scornful eye,
"Their colour is a diabolic die."
Remember, *Christians*, *Negros*, black as *Cain*,
May be refin'd, and join th' angelic train.

To the Right Honourable Phillis Wheatley
By Natalie Gonzalez

'Twas mercy brought you from your pagan land?
Mercy, poet, holds no dagger in hand.
There's a God, and His Son a Savior too:
Long before you knew Him, He of you knew.
For all-seeing is the Holy Father's divine eye
"Of Mine own image create, I."
No longer shalt thou live in gilded chain,
Thou art, in thine own right, angelic, Black as Cain.

Ode To Cinnamon

By Branden Ray Garcia

Cinnamon is simply not a spice,
Not a staple to some kind of recipe
for guaranteed delight or happiness,
but rather guaranteed struggle, turmoil, and frustration.

No one can choose to be cinnamon.
Birthed through gnarled bark and then peeled off
Aesthetics of skin declared as rough on us, but soft on others
A seared brown color forever baked into their skin.

Forcibly pounded and grinded for many a years
to become less than the natural state
Yet still claimed as second best to sugar,
used to make up for what cinnamon cannot sate
Brown loose powder manages to make many choke if alone
Never allowed to be enjoyed unless without the presence of a foreign other
Seen as a curse for many, some manage to turn it into a blessing.

The promised land of the mind blessed by young mothers and sons at stoves
Small canisters of cinnamon labeled as patience, adversity, and persistence
Self-love learned from the fragrance of one's culture
Scarred history of colonized ancestors scarred skin
Forced to peel the bark off themselves
Yet, We find solace.

Not defined by wispy tendrils threatened to be
burned by the world
but rather definitions of what being brown means to many
 To be cinnamon is challenging, bold, and reinventive,
A spice of so much flavor and identity that it overpowers all other flavors and fragrances
No pairing of spices can overcome the perseverance of cinnamon
Unless mixed with the right combination of love, technique, and experience,
It seems cinnamon is no longer the spice it was, but the tree it originated from.

Forever emboldened, strong, and able.

Kudos to My First Love

By Lala C-B (Alana Cooks-Beeks)

Oh to America, my home land I say, sarcastically.
I truly mean oh to my momma who raised and praised me.
Protected me without rejecting me.
When I reflect I see her in the stands.
She's never not been in my master plan.

Where there are stereotypes and hurtful fights,
plights that added distance.
She sees me in herself, wishes and gives me wealth.
And even those words that are left unspoken I am still left with a token a gift.
I truly got lucky.

My mother so strong. Who made sure my base could embrace the blades of life.
My mother who cried and stood with pride and showed me I am as to be described, a beautiful black queen. That no man can stop me.

As it is true the apple doesn't fall far from the tree. That's why I'm top quality. She expects the best of me.

There's just one thing that I can say.
Momma can I get 20 bucks?
Please?
I luv you!

Ode to Dad

By Simone Jenkins

You're my hero
Dad,
You took your two children in
We win,
We have the best father ever.

Dad,
You're my forever.
I will never forget
That you raised us
No regret
Took us out of the possibility
Of being fostered
All of my fears were conquered.

Dad,
You sacrificed
To be there for us,
Everything you did for us
You did for you too.
You made sure we had food
And there I show gratitude.

Dad,
You wish you could hold me
In your arms right now,
But because of you,
To be amazing I vow.

I'm multi talented
Never have time
But with you I balance it.

Dad,
I'm growing up
Don't cry
You did everything well,
You tried.
You didn't fail.

Dad,
You're raising me right
My grades are tight.
I have no fear.
My bright future is near.

Dad,
You have inspired me
To be like you,
But times three
No matter what we go through.
Having a teenage girl must be tough,
Yelling at me with your voice all rough.

Dad,
I still want to be like you,
Even after I wed.
You'll never be replaced,
Even after the challenges we face.
Even when I was younger,
I knew you were working
So we never had hunger.
Before we had a stepmother,
I would wonder,

What would it be like for my dad to be happy?
God answered that for me gladly.
Even though you're not by yourself,
To you I will never say farewell.

I love you

∼

Ode to Jump Rope

By Branden Ray Garcia

Running fast, legs tangle as we do what we were taught
From giggling warm playground sands to somber cold back alley gangs
We all seem to double-dutch unless we'd want to be caught
Grievances would never fade, bloodstains seep, stuck in the dingy carpet of the late
Eyes as reflective as our last moments praying we wouldn't end up decayed
Remembering how giddy school kids seem to parade
Innocent thoughts flowing around for the day
Day shines on as all seems to be revealed
Jump Ropes come alive and ashy knees fall onto the pavement and peel.

Pay attention to the boom, bang, and pows
Yet, spoken secrets, and jump the ropes that don't allow
Vital life skill indubitably taught, careful to position yourself not to be caught
 Slips and slides make us fall into the ground
Jump Rope always slaps those who aren't adaptable
Curls became tangled, bracelets and rings jangled, ammo fell and bodies dismantled.
Get up. Move. Or else be trampled.
None of us came out with hope in the Star Banner which was spangled
Yet many of us that night would fall and become the night sky as stars, dangled.

I stepped on someone's back to escape.
Double-dutching over the dead bodies of the party on Washington Street
Bullets swirl around us, man-made balance made to weed out those who had drank Coronas
I don't pray to God, but to my Mami and the two little pigtailed girls swirling the ropes of fate
The pavement they stand on, I stomp; Each foot down sculpting my grave
We can only hope our tears moisten the ground, allowing flowers to bloom through our flesh.

Ode to the former misfits

By Aaliyah Beato-Hubbard

We were the background characters that had background conversations ones you can see but not hear
We cursed when our parents weren't around because it made us feel like we were in control of something.
We skipped class and hid in bathrooms
It's me, do you remember?
I looked at my phone <u>still no reply</u>
Life has changed dearly since we left.
We all went our separate ways

Maybe it's the separation anxiety that's not letting me let go; She doesn't let anything go. She holds on to the past and present moment as if we could die without it.
So I have to write this poem to move on, to try to forget as you have forgotten me
I guess I just want to know if you're doing well if you are alright without me.
I hope you know I still hide in bathrooms and yell lyrics to songs in empty halls that have our memories plastered on the walls.

I'm here remembering the times we disturbed class as dares that we would never back down from, and ran from the teachers who saw us.
I hope you know I'm still here
I still sing the song of the misfits as a solo act
I know you guys found your homes, your boxes, and I hope you don't let people put you in just one. You guys are extraordinary and as you guys shine

I will be here, in a box left at the back of a storage room memory.
I know you guys wanted me to shine but I'm ok; you guys can be
stars and I will be the night sky that once held you up until you
learned how to hold yourself. Just here holding onto where I
come from.

I hope you never forget where you came from even if the
memory of me isn't there with it
We were misfits and now you guys fit
I won't fit
I am a misfit.

∼

True African Beauty

By Rebekah Davilmar

The reflection of our Ancestors of African Descent: They were at least told once that their black wasn't beautiful.

     My black is beautiful.

Ever since I was young
I was told that my
Hair and skin didn't matter
I was told to change my hair
Because it wasn't "appropriate" for school.
I thought the idea of having nice
And long hair was to iron it
To straighten it and get rid of my curls
Because those curls weren't a form of beauty.

They didn't fit in the standard of beauty
My big curly Afro hair wasn't beautiful enough.
That was my norm, that is what I knew.

I was addicted to that fancy long blonde straight hair
Because I was told that this was beautiful
I was told that my afro didn't matter that I should try
This perm and that perm in order to hide my curls.

     For years I abused and tortured it

Blonde hair barbies never taught me how to love the brown in me

In society we are told that brown-skinned girls don't get depression but yet, they get silenced.

Cocoa brown girls who have to face society every day and be tough
Because no matter how good they straighten their hair
Their good is still not good enough.
I sit and ponder not knowing the way society portrays this form of beauty when it comes to black African natural hair.

See
My hair defines me.
It can show you where I've been and where I'm going.

It's important to me sometimes I am able
To express myself through the different
Styles that I do.
My hair is curly it is dark with
Not only thickness but strength.

You see, I like the way my stands twist, turn and curl uptight
Rebelling against society's demand that lay flat without a fight
There is heritage, a lineage with soul-stirring stories to share
Our skin holds history and the story isn't over yet

Look up.
Magically our hair curls

My hair is just like me: Beautiful, resilient, and full of pride.

My black is beautiful.

Years of being told that I wasn't the standard for beauty
That my blackness isn't beautiful that my skin isn't beautiful
There's multiple forms of beauty

There's not just one ideal picture of beauty
There is no ugly in our imperfection
Our skin absorbs sunlight, Our hair defies gravity.

> We got this melanin and we gotta wear it
> With pride.

You took our darkness for granted don't forget how we shine
How the sun finds comfort in our skin.
When society tries to pin light versus dark skin we remind them that every shade of chocolate is Divinely crafted.

> Black Girl Magic is more than a
> HASHTAG IT IS A
> MOVEMENT
> A STATEMENT

Like Maxine Waters, gaining Our power moving through this world unapologetically Degree-holding with our head held high.
Her free and natural hair wrapped in a protective style.
Black girl you better recognize we are Trail Blazers

> We are trendsetters
> We are style benders
> And now it's my turn
> I'll make my own mark
> I'll Love my own skin

> My black is beautiful.

When i define my own standards, who needs to blend in?

> And remember that
> YOU.
> Are Everything!

Empowerment

My black is beautiful.
Ever since I was young
I was told that my
skin didn't matter

My black is beautiful

The Mirror

By Ethan Mitchell

The mirror
Picks and prods at the pores on your skin
Making you count calories as you deface yourself with insecurity
Adding pounds on the silvery surface
Distorting Destroying and causing Decay

Telling you you aren't good enough for anything; not even for it.

It lies, that mirror-
But you knew that already
That it never tells you what you want to hear
Yet, it still deceives you
You're infatuated; obsessed.

No matter how hard you try, you're drawn to it
a moth to a flame

It wouldn't matter if you shattered it
For it is eternal
Without beginning or ending
Try as you may, you will never rid yourself of it
You've chosen your fate; entangled in your own delusions
Creating false realities that never heal your own shattered psyche

It only projects what you feel

Every time you go to the mirror, you're once again surprised.

Thus, you should never trust the mirror
For the mirror only lies.

But you knew that already.

An Ode to my Errors

By Emily Wu

To all my errors,
whether you are a stumble, slip-up, or even a crash, I thank you.

I say "Thank You" because you have taught me how to grow like a seed in my grandmother's garden, springing quickly towards the sky.

You have made me strong,

                    a lion in the middle of a city.

Not only surviving but thriving.

I'm not afraid to try, because you, error, are inevitable. Though you may try, you cannot stop me. You are only there so that I can succeed later. You are only a mistake, anyways.

You, error, have a purpose -
although I don't often see it in the moment. If it weren't for you, who would I be?

Ode to Money
By Rhoda Kaddu

Man has given you power.
Your existence expands my horizons and limits my opportunities. Your absences exhaust my mental but your presence provides me with stability.
To be the cause of my deterioration but be the potential pinnacle of my success.
The common denominator in my consciousness' greedy tendency. Wields a great influence on a moral compass.
A reason to mentally and physically strain our bodies. I crave your abundance.

Money

The root of all evil is the solution to all my life's miseries.

Money

Its value worthless but its presence made necessary.

Money

Simultaneously decreasing and improving the quality of life.
My favorite worldly possession,
my favorite vice

Money

Ode to Dreams
By Ari-Renzi-Surprenant

You are an unfinished masterpiece
One without completion
Remember, within you lives endless inspiration.
Eternal beauty hidden within your murky depths.
How I long to know you.
To feel your sweet caresses,
As you sing to me
All the secrets of the universe.
The shortness of life
So many unanswered questions
That I may never know the answer to.
An artist's work unfinished,
The book left unread.
Oh, how I wish I knew you.
But, in truth, you know me.
More than anyone ever could.
You are me.
And I am you.

Ode to That Which Cannot Be Known

By Sarah Saeed

Stoic as the night sky
Alight in the stars' meditative splendor
I ponder that
Which cannot be known.

I do not bow to god above
For the fire of living
Is within, crackling, creeping
Into my bloodstream, wet and warm
yet I do not
Know where it comes from

Who breathes heat into hearth
Who pestles the sky's ice into
Ash, fine as it falls,

Whose slumber brings suffering
Barren, but for the bones of what once was
Whose wake warrants

Forgiveness

We feed and forget
Who is it that we forgive so easily?

I lie unconscious, trusting
That such a spirit will maintain
The reverberation of my chest

That cavernous chamber that

Rises like the tides
Blind in both dark and light I
Wander, I ponder, that
Which cannot be known.

Ode to Mofongo

By Branden Ray Garcia

As I strip my two pale plantains of its skins, I can't help but think of what you did
Slicing up what remains of this Puerto Rican staple,
Chop me up into little bits and choose what you declare as able
Boiling it down within the deep depths of a heavily greased oil-filled pan
Turn me into something malleable,
and planned.

You wish to skin the sweet, yet Black skin of a nicely aged platano
Declaring it is rotten, not sweet. A malady to the dream dinner you compose
Demonize the very transformative, protective gift blessed that send souls flying
There's always a moment of silence before the plantain starts frying.
Starts up slow but grease will blow
Oil takes no prisoners, but I'll try to say this slow
Oil sizzles and threatens back
Identities, pride, and ancestral ties have been erased, trying to make one lack

You give no response.
Blank stare, disregard, I dream to end it.
My heart's been bended.
Oil pops, you've stopped, I'm unattended
Mere words make you deny me, blind as the night

But I can't stand that, so you know what? Yeah I'm not blended

I'm not any mix you've ever seen
No label, or tag
Yet Slap the Chiquita Banana sticker onto this teen
Only Latino to you as my ancestors beg for honesty,
A platano is still just a platano to you, ignoring the skin
Because to you, I and Latino went hand in hand,
Colorblind to the artistry of my family's complexion, a subtle attack.

However, the best part about mofongo is that it matters what's inside
A basic taste when first fried
Any lie or truth can be used to give it life
But the contents in the makeshift cup make it sublime
Molding me for who you wanted me to be
Turned me alive, and ready to see.

I gaze upon the mofongo in my hands
My ancestors reach out and I can feel the blood of distant lands
Habichuelas flood my creation and I am whole
Beans of distant ancestral past fill my mofongo
The feeling of realization and content that cannot be stole
And I'll make sure any man that holds my heart cannot steal my soul.

Oda a Mofongo

Por Branden Ray Garcia

Traducido Por Eddie Maisonet

Mientras le quito la piel a mis dos pálidos plátanos, no puedo evitar pensar en lo que hiciste
Rebanado lo que queda de este alimento básico puertorriqueño,
Córtame en pedacitos y elige lo que declares como capaz
Hervirlo en las profundidades profundas de una sartén llena de aceite muy engrasada
Conviérteme en algo maleable
 y planeado.

Desea despellejar la piel dulce pero negra de un plátano bien añejado.
Declarando que está podrido, no dulce. Una enfermedad a la cena de ensueño que compones
Demonizar el regalo protector y transformador bendito que envía almas a volar.
Siempre hay un momento de silencio antes de que el plátano comience a freírse.
Arranca lento pero la grasa se derrama
El aceite no toma prisioneros, pero intentaré decir esto despacio
El aceite chisporrotea y amenaza
Se han borrado las identidades, el orgullo y los lazos ancestrales, tratando de hacer una falta.

No das ninguna respuesta.
Mirada en blanco, desprecio, sueño con terminarlo.
Mi corazón se ha doblado.
Pops de aceite, te detuviste, estoy desatendido
Meras palabras te hacen negarme, ciego como la noche
Pero no puedo soportar eso, entonces, ¿sabes qué? Sí, no estoy mezclado

No soy ninguna mezcla que hayas visto
Sin etiqueta o rótulo
Sin embargo, abofetéale la pegatina de Chiquita Banana a este adolescente

Solo latino para ti como mis ancestros suplican honestidad,
Un plátano sigue siendo solo un plátano para ti, ignorando la piel
Porque para ti Latino y yo fuimos de la mano,
Daltónico al arte de la tez de mi familia, un ataque sutil.

Sin embargo, la mejor parte del mofongo es que importa lo que hay dentro
Un sabor básico cuando se fríe por primera vez.
Cualquier mentira o verdad puede usarse para darle vida.
Pero el contenido de la taza improvisada lo hace sublime
Moldeándome para quien querías que fuera
Me volvió vivo y listo para ver.

Miro el mofongo en mis manos
Mis ancestros se acercan y puedo sentir la sangre de tierras lejanas
Habichuelas inunden mi creación y estoy entero
Frijoles de lejano pasado ancestral llenan mi mofongo
La sensación de realización y contenido que no se puede robar.
Y me aseguraré de que cualquier hombre que tenga mi corazón no pueda robar mi alma.

~

An Ode To Fighting

By Adrianna Diaz

Everyday is a rollercoaster of fighting to stay alive
All my days on replay proud that I've survived
Surprised my boxing gloves aren't ripped the way I fight through life
My social depression might hit me with a left but I always find a way to punch it with my right

Jab, cross, hook - I will never stop fighting
All this pain in my mind so I spill my feelings out on these pages and include my thoughts in every word when I'm writing

Even with tears in my eyes I'm still standing

People always want to see me down but I've won every single round
So that just proves that I'm a champion
Some think I'm lying but not all scars are visible
I remember depression beat me once and his name was clinical

Mood swings here and mood swings there
But there's fire in my soul and when you stare into my eyes you can see the glare
Some days I might break down but it's ok to be weak
I can fall down six times but I will always get up times three
Some days my heart can feel cold but it's ok to just freeze

And think... and breathe

I have to accept that the wounds, bruises, and scars are what make me, me
I will always be a champion, I will always be a fighter

An Ode to Depression
By Adrianna Diaz

I am dancing with my thoughts
I linger with my mind
It's always my head versus my heart
People who sleep through the light don't know
how it feels to live in the dark
Step back ... forward... step back... then I trip
I fall but then I think getting confused
between
these emotions
Too attached to the water I can't even focus on
the motion
I can't swim but I am drowning
deep in this ocean
that no one seems to notice
yelling...screaming...shouting
but because of you no one can hear me
In a room filled with hundreds of people
but only you can see me
Maybe my presence isn't enough
now no one will ever feel me
Monsters hiding in my closet
but
I think that they are friendly
At least they listen to all my pain while they
hear me cry and hold me gently
Fire within my soul but I can't feel the heat
Blinded from the darkness what if I never see
My heart is as cold as ice and I can't feel my feet

Copy and pasting my life away but having depression is the mind pressing repeat
Over thinking Over thinking I'm on repeat
I'm on repeat, I can not sleep, I'm on repeat
Sometimes I hate you
sometimes I love you
but thank you depression

Ode to Sappho: On Heaven

By Natalie Gonzalez

> *Now, while we dance*
> *Come here to us*
> *gentle Gaiety,*
> *Revelry, Radiance*
> *and you, Muses*
> *with lovely hair*

Was there ever a time when my eyes
Could hold Hers for more than a breath?
Shame, that we fear our doom too much
To swim in its honeyed depths.

> I find myself wondering what it would be like,
> How it might feel to lick the sap that drips from trees
> And not notice when my teeth ached from the taste

But sweet Knowledge belongs to his paradise,
Deemed too powerful for mortal hands to touch.
Yet, if I were to sink into one constellation,
Trace my skin along the surface of one midnight river of divinity,
Would any star in that infinite lake of heaven
Compare to the chiming of her precious laughter?

> Scheherazade herself could not weave her words fine enough,
> Could not spin a tale of such drunken silk
> As to compare to the softness of Her smile.

And as the last rays of rosey twilight give way
To the Huntress's careful silver gaze
The imperfect is divine once more
And Love, newly born, sets Her feet upon the shore.

Ode to Ebonics

By Shirley Jones Luke

My first tongue   before the language of my ancestors   was scraped

from it   heard   in a home of bluster & blues   the history

of a people   ma sang   African spirituals mixed with New World hymns   dad spoke with a

southern twang   lost when he yelled

My grandmother   ma's momma   French West Indies born

pure French   the colonizer's tongue   I couldn't say "three" when I was a little girl   It sounded

like "tree"

a combination of three generations   who depended on me

to lead the family   on a new path   away from European egos

& Stay true to my heritage   I'm finna go to bed   I'm fixin' to mail this here letter   What had

happened was   Where he be at? Arraya hungry? What you mean?!   I dunno   it's all

figurative not just

relative   idioms   street lingo   bravado   show me your black

tongue   dipped in melanin & called a sin   voices echoing

from the past   infusing the diaspora of today   my first tongue

seeks the language   of my ancestors   the language of me

END NOTE

∼

There's beauty in this book.

Some surprising beauty, and humor, and passion on these pages.

Fierceness.

Edgy moments.

Love.

Contempt.

Admiration.

Some rage here and there, sometimes hidden behind a metaphor, sometimes not.

Ideas you didn't know about, or things you knew once when you were a teenager, and forgot.

In the spring of 2020, in the midst of a pandemic lockdown and social justice protests, I was working on *Friends & Anemones: Ocean Poems for Children*. Between emails about illustrations, page count, and the news, my mind wandered to another project. Most of us at the Loft are white. What about an anthology that reaches out to our local Black community. Could we organize that?

At first I talked myself out of it, because it was intimidating. I didn't know the right people to get that done.

But I went to some webinars about race, including one by the Brown Bookshelf. Between learning about microagressions and colorism, speakers said that talking about race would be awkward. And that's okay.

And I thought, I can totally do awkward! That's right up my alley.

I started (awkwardly) reaching out to the literal handful of people I know who are Black or Latine writers. Thank you Lisa Stringfellow, Janet Bates, and Anika Aldaumy Denise for being at the top of that short list. They helped me find the editors. Thank you to Shirley Jones Luke and Eddie Maisonet for saying yes to being editors, and helping me find the poets. Shirley and Eddie reached out to their communities, and slowly the Writers' Loft Press gmail filled up with glorious poems written by teens of color. "My English teacher gave me your email ..." and "I saw a post on Instagram about a poetry anthology ..."

Each poem was so *intense*, as teenagers tend to be.

These kids didn't have to write these poems, they chose to. They didn't have to stick with this project over the course of more than a year, either.

Some of them are in college now.

Some of them are still in high school.

None of them wrote specifically about the pandemic, but it hovers in the background.

All of them wrote with their hearts.

I wasn't sure if I should put in this note. ODES OF US is not about me, the white organizer also hovering in the background, it's about the 'us' in the title—the poets.

But in the interest of awkwardness, authenticity, and the truth, it's good for our greater Loft community to know where this book came from, and why. And how we can all keep using our platforms to make things better.

Thank you for reading the work of these brave young writers.

Next time, when we are able to include these writers in our future anthologies, because they are part of our community now we won't need an awkward note at the end.

—Kristen Wixted, Publisher, Project Manager

OTHER WRITERS' LOFT PRESS ANTHOLOGIES

∼

Firsts

∼

An Assortment Of Animals

∼

Friends & Anemones

www.ingramcontent.com/pod-product-compliance
Lightning Source LLC
Chambersburg PA
CBHW030458010526
44118CB00011B/1000